Nocturnal Wanderings

Jason Zapata

Nocturnal Wanderings

Copyright © 2013 Jason Zapata
All rights reserved.

ISBN: 0988911809
ISBN-13: 978-0-9889118-0-2

Editor: Jason Stershic
Cover Design: Christopher J. Hughes
Back Cover Author Photo: Lyndsey Hughes
Page Layout/Design: Jason Stershic

Published by Spectyr Media, Ltd.
Printed by CreateSpace, An Amazon.com Company

Available from Amazon.com, CreateSpace.com, other retail outlets, Kindle and online stores

Contact the Author
zapata.wordsmith@gmail.com
www.jasonzapata.com

DEDICATION

To my loving parents, Efrain and Anna Zapata.

INTRODUCTION

Where did all of this come from, all of these words and stories? I look at the collection of poetry that is "Nocturnal Wanderings" and the answer definitely lies in the past. Many of these poems were inspired by my earlier experiences. The writing was very raw, and it would be years before any of it was ready to see the light of day.

Writing became a permanent facet of my life the moment my father handed me a copy of "The Elfstones of Shannara" by Terry Brooks. I devoured the novel at the age of six.

Tolkien followed shortly afterwards. Then Anne Rice, whose vampires, witches, and atmospheric settings were the inspiration behind many of the poems I penned. The final literary influence of my youth was Neil Gaiman. I remember going to Comics on the Green in Scranton every payday to purchase another "Sandman" graphic novel. Of all the stories I've read, it's the tale of Morpheus that resonates strongest with me.

I also remember the many hours I spent with the Metal Militia, a motley crew of friends and musicians who introduced me to the world of heavy metal. James Heitfield, Ozzy Osbourne, and Jonathan Davis were the songwriters I followed. They sang of wars, inner demons, and the supernatural. Science fiction and horror movies were thrown into the mix as well. I gravitated towards all these themes as a restless young man.

Though at times I try to deny it, I was and remain a hopeless romantic. Countless times I've gone for a walk under the starry night sky. Those moonlit strolls were usually spurred on by some Irish ghost story I read or someone I was longing for at the time. This tendency to write romantic yarns isn't completely contradictory. I still infuse enough elements of the supernatural to make these poems my own.

What about the poets? Shouldn't there be poets who inspired me? Yes. There was obviously some influence from Edgar Allan Poe. Samuel Taylor Coleridge also made an impression with his "Rime of the Ancient Mariner." Maybe a splash of Lord Byron, but it's always really been about music and novels for me.

Years passed with the bulk of the poetry in "Nocturnal Wanderings" residing on my computer. Unpolished. Unseen. As time passed, my writer's voice developed. Creative writing courses and poetry workshops sharpened my skills. I looked over my work and felt confident I could make it worthy of publication.

Enter Jason Stershic. Old friend and editor who took on the arduous task of helping assemble the book. All the poems I had crafted up to that point were gathered and reviewed. Many times. An elaborate spreadsheet tracked the number of rewrites and noted what work was to be saved or cut altogether. There were some heated debates over edits and cuts. Writers are always too critical of their work. Jason was quick to point this out and resurrected many of the poems I tried to scrap. Being a writer and already familiar with my work, his aid was indispensable.

Gradually, the project reached its conclusion. The rough edges from poems written nearly a decade ago were now smooth. And as I looked over my work once more, it retained all of its nostalgia without sacrificing the skills I've developed. "Nocturnal Wanderings" is a poetry collection and a time capsule at the same time. I'm reminded of all the memories, people, and stories of my past whenever I flip through its pages.

Table of Contents

Path I

3	|	Monastery In The Southern Wood
6	|	A Question Of Faith
7	|	The Man
8	|	2084
9	|	Villain In The Villanelle
10	|	Atlas Walks Away
12	|	His Rules
13	|	My Portrait
14	|	Out Of Exile
15	|	Open Hand, Clenched Fist
16	|	Requiem
17	|	A Thousand Evil Souls
18	|	Ghosts Of You And Me
19	|	Anam Cara
20	|	The Walk
21	|	Dryad's Smile
22	|	The Sea, She, And The Sailor
23	|	At Wars' End
24	|	Widow In The Window
25	|	Control

Path II

29	|	Voodoo Queen
30	|	In Her Grip
31	|	All In Her Name
32	|	My Shadow
34	|	End Not Ready For
35	|	Dance Of The Dead
36	|	Child Of A Dark Prometheus
37	|	We Will Not Fade Away
38	|	Damned Son Of Abraham
39	|	Wheat Field With Crows
40	|	A Night In Avalon
42	|	The Dawn
44	|	Those Good Ole Times
45	|	A Devil's Lament
46	|	My Redeemer
47	|	Just A Shove
48	|	Boogie Man
49	|	Mykoshakan Prison

Path III

53 | Winter's Love
54 | Outsider's Eyes
56 | It's All Right I'm All Right
57 | Until I Awake
58 | Asking Why
59 | The Waiter
60 | Nihilio Ex Nihilio
61 | Sun And Moon
62 | It Looks Like Rain
64 | The Words
65 | Tin Man
66 | Free
67 | Pee Wee Gone Mad
68 | A Redemption You Don't Deserve
70 | Unaware
72 | Familiar Madness
73 | Grand Scheme of Things
75 | Ongoing Story of Death And The Wandering Jew

PATH I

The Monastery in the Southern Wood

I am the architect of my own grim folly.
A being tormented by lasting memories
Of a cursed place from which I cannot seek refuge.
Even in the depths of sleep…
The memory is always with me.

I was hunting in the forest south of my village.
Forgoing the worn trail, I waded through fern,
Past ancient moss encrusted oaks and maples.
I remember hearing voices. Distant chanting
That cowed the woods around me into silence.

No longer was I concerned with the hunt.
My sole intent was to leave those still woods,
Until I glimpsed it through the maze of trees.
Camouflaged in overgrowth stood a structure,
A derelict and forsaken monastery.

Anyone with sense wouldn't have approached.
Yet all the same I did. Without any explanation
I reached for a heavy door entwined in ivy.
And paused. Frozen by an unearthly breeze
As it passed through my outstretched fingers.

Guardedly, I explored the monastery's foyer.
Dead leaves swirled across the wooden floor,
Which nature gradually reclaimed with rot.
Scant light crept through broken stained glass,
And I was all too aware of the cold and darkness.

I recall beholding the blasphemous artifacts then.
My eyes had gazed upward and spotted them.
Hanging motionlessly from web-covered rafters
Was a set of disturbing tapestries. Lurid images
Which told a macabre story from left to right.

The first depicted a beggar with a wooden staff
Asking for food from monks dining at a table.
There was a grim revelation in the second tapestry.
The beggar was a leper the monks refused to aid,
Piety and Christian generosity had been forsworn.

The third showed the leper holding his staff,
Before him, the monks lay stricken and dying.
The final tapestry had the leper sitting
At the head of the table, dead skeletal monks
Kept him company as he ate his meal.

What evil to be housed in a monastery, I thought.

Again I heard disjointed voices, but much closer.
And with a chilling certainty, I then understood.
It was singing. More accurately it was prayer.
The afternoon vespers being sung as they would
In any monastery the faithful visit.

Vespers heard in the confines of that cursed place
Provided no comfort. This was no house of God.
Why did I allow the vespers to entrance me?
I fell victim to their sirens call while knowing
They could only end in a dirge.

My leaden feet carried me towards a hallway.
Gradually I became aware of desecrated icons,
Ruined faces of the Mother and Savior.
Their loving visages were either slashed or torn
And encrusted with fetid filth.

I forced myself to suppress shudders of revulsion,
While an eternity passed in the increasing darkness.
Desperately I maintained control of my imagination,
Preventing it from conjuring images of spirits
As phantom breezes raised the hair on my arms.

Finally, I saw illumination at the end of the hall.
Within an oratory faintly lit by remnants of candles,
I saw some monks whose backs were turned to me.
Frail forms in threadbare habits knelt in prayer.
Who were these monks and why were they here?

An abrupt silence followed as the vespers ceased
And a lone monk rose. It was an eerie motion.
"Ask the Leper," he rasped with a disgusted voice.
Then all the monks stood and turned toward me.
"Heaven help me," I cried.

What shadows their tattered robes provided,
Couldn't conceal the decomposition I beheld.
"My brothers and I would join in your prayer,
But our voices have lost all efficaciousness.
Please, won't you stay for the Compline?"

I fled without answering the question.
Hooded wraiths followed after in the darkness,
Their closing footsteps fueled my terrified flight.
I looked over my shoulder the whole way,
And only stopped when I was back home.

Memories of that day haunt me still. Many years later,
During long watches of the night, I hear their prayers.
I remember the tapestries and I understand their curse.
The leper has damned the monks to an unlife of service
In the forsaken monastery in the southern wood.

A Question of Faith

The Saint sat next to me, golden halo overhead.
She towered over me. A gorgeous monument
Donned in a gray business suit that made
Her apple red hair stand out even more.

She opened a pack of Marlboro lights,
Pulled one out and lit up casually.
Between long, delicate fingers
She held the cigarette and turned to me.

"Are you ever going to get over this?"

I said nothing. I couldn't find the words while
Those divinity-filled eyes bore into my own.
She waited patiently, smoking,
Flicking the ashes of her cigarette to the side.

After a while, her thin lips parted
Blowing smoke and forming a humoring smile.
The Saint pulled back her gray suit sleeves,
Revealing two heavily bandaged wrists.

"Stigmata?" I asked wearily.

She shook her head, "It's carpal tunnel syndrome.
A self-inflicted curse through playing piano
Despite the pain I feel. It's suffering which defines me.
How does your suffering define you?"

She was gone. Her question hung in the air,
Like the last wisps of her cigarette smoke.
Am I ever going to get over this?
It's a question of faith I cannot answer.

The Man

The man curses softly for he knows it's time to rise,
Viewing the dawn with bloodshot weary eyes,
He struggles to get up it seems harder as he tries,
Another day has begun.

The man braces himself for the struggle he expects,
Fragile hopes and dreams he has sworn to protect,
Will crumble to dust with a moment's neglect,
The day is far from done.

From twilight to starlight,
From dusk to dawn,
He battles relentlessly through the years.
Ever haunted by the possible
Realization of his worst fears.

The days they become months,
Those months turn into years,
All this time he never questions his cause.
Never surrenders to the doubts which
Would make all others pause.

The man doesn't bother to lie to himself or pretend
All too aware of the hardships he must contend.
Knowing he burns the candle at both ends
As day wanes to night.

But the man shows no sign of surrendering yet.
And through every bitter battle that is met,
The setting sun doesn't herald the dusk of regret,
But the promise of another fight.

2084

An electric blue glow fills dilated eyes
As a singular ideology stirs instilled belief.
The Ministry of Security's proclamations
Are televised totalitarianism, describing
A world of color-coated terror, displayed
For all the faithful citizenry to see.
Allies and enemies change with every week
Never do the people question what it means -
They're all programmed to believe.

"WAR IS PEACE
FREEDOM IS SLAVERY
IGNORANCE IS STRENGTH"

What they know is what they think they know.
They know not.

Traitors were rooted out among the citizenry,
Terrorist sympathizers who questioned the law.
Dissentious voices were muted and reformed
Into Americans who wouldn't question authority.
If not for the expanded powers of the Patriot Act
These deviants may have remained at large.
The first step in securing the great American nation
Was ensuring every American be watched at all times.
Americans are programmed to believe.

"WAR IS PEACE
FREEDOM IS SLAVERY
IGNORANCE IS STRENGTH"

What they know is what they think they know.
They know not.

Villain in the Villanelle

Don't blame me for mortal design.
I'll not be your scapegoat anymore,
This Hell you've created is not mine.

Man needs no temptation to cross the line.
Their faults and crimes they readily ignore,
Don't blame me for mortal design.

It's repeated with Carneal and Columbine.
Cruelty begets death as it always has before,
This Hell you've created is not mine.

Persecution repeated throughout time.
You lay Jim Crow and Auschwitz at my door,
Don't blame me for mortal design.

Beziers, Peking, and Beslan mark your decline.
Assured in continued genocide and holy war,
This Hell you've created is not mine.

I take no pleasure in calling you mine.
Never have I had so many of you here before.
Mortals, don't blame me for your design,
This Hell you've created is not mine.

Atlas Walks Away

You never stopped to ask yourself if it was fair,
Leaving obligations for me to shoulder alone.
Taking for granted I would always be there,
The Atlas to hold your troubled world aloft.
A responsibility I have come to forswear.

As I struggled under the weight of all this,
The double standards became obvious to me.
Promises I honored you callously dismissed.
The stress that bore down on my shoulders grew
And I questioned why such a world should exist.

But it is not your fault.
You are no better or worse
Than everyone else is.

Of course you can only be as good
As the world which grinds upon
My shoulders allows you to be.

But this doesn't have to be my destiny.

The time for honesty and answers overdue,
I now questioned the worth of this arrangement.
Didn't I have a right to ask more of you?
Guilt was expected from my every request,
Until what little faith I had was subdued.

It was then I rose from my bruised unfeeling knee.
And the world you thought would never change,
Was destroyed by my defiance against this absurdity.
I accepted that you would brand me a traitor,
Your villain in this self fulfilled prophecy.

But it was not my fault.
I was no better or worse
Than everyone else was.

Of course I could only be as good
As the world which grinded upon
My shoulders allowed me to be.

But this was never meant to be my destiny.

Pitiless I will leave you to your deserved disarray,
Kneeling amongst the ruins of everything you knew.
The broken look in your eyes no longer had sway.
My revenge in this story is my redemption
That enduring Atlas can finally walk away.

His Rules

Armored men scream their battle cry,
Heard by victors and those doomed to die.
The iron clad warriors struggle and strain,
Driven to see their enemies slain.

Men battle atop steel covered steeds,
Will their acts be remembered as heroic deeds?
The dead and God know, neither will say,
Bound to the law they will not betray.

Honor your land, honor your father,
Slay the enemy who is your brother.

Axes cleave through heavy chain mail,
Arrows plummet in a deadly hail.
Shields become battered by vicious blows,
Fallen bodies left for ravenous crows.

A helmeted skull is crushed by a mace,
Blood runs down a dead mans face.
Mothers left weeping with nothing to say,
Lost their sons to the rules they had to obey.

Honor your land, honor your father,
Slay the enemy who is your brother.

Though kingdoms and people change with the ages,
War continues to fill history's blood soaked pages.
Unknowing men death's set of tools,
To keep secure his set of rules.

Honor your land, honor your father,
Slay the enemy who is your brother.

My Portrait

This portrait is mine,
Though it looks nothing like me.
A reflection of my soul.
It grows worse with every deed
And worse with every day.
It grows worse while I do not.
This portrait – must remain unseen.
My soul's mirror displayed in conceit,
But veiled so I cannot see…
What has become of me?
Golden hair's gone grey,
Youthful flesh turned putrescent.
And my baleful eyes serve,
As windows to a vacant dwelling.
This portrait is mine,
Though it looks nothing like me.
How I wish this art to be false.

Out of Exile

I can hear your voice on the other side,
But only words travel across this divide.
Can't you sense I'm becoming desperate,
To demolish this wall keeping us separate?

You speak of blissful union and matrimony,
But such comforting words sound so phony.
When I pace this side of the wall alone,
Glimpsing you through cracks in the stone.

You've strayed from me all this time,
Hidden behind this wall I cannot climb.
I cannot tell you all the things I mean to say,
When this wall still stands in my way.

A wall to divide love and hate.
A wall built up by the hands of fate.
What sides do we represent
And who has made that judgment?

What do you want of me, my dear,
For this wall to stand or disappear?
Only when it's a rocky pile
Can I show you the way out of exile.

Open Hand, Clenched Fist

My hands are flesh and bone copies of yours, father.
Splinters and scars are the landscape from palm to finger
Skin coarsened with calluses, showing signs of weather
Through the work of time. Strong hands. Working hands.

But your hands have built things your entire life.
Family, home, opportunities for me,
I've yet to build anything.
My empty hands can only clench with anger.
Shaking your head, you say to me:

"An open hand can choose to hold a hammer,
An open hand can choose to hold a plow,
An open hand can choose to hold those dear,
But a clenched fist cannot hold anything."

My hands are flesh and bone copies of yours, father.
But the only thing they can hold is anger.
I look at my clenched fists, knuckles turned white.
Rigormortis has set in.

Requiem

I know my candle has burned too fast
Despite my best efforts I cannot last.
My heart beats slow within my chest
Telling me its time to give it a rest.

Cease resisting and let myself go under,
Abandon this world I hold in wonder.
I will close strained and weary eyes
And rest in peace where shadows lie.

The wind speaks through the bare trees,
Not with the renewal of a spring breeze.
I can hear the rustle of great wings,
It's time to be at peace with all things.

A Thousand Evil Souls

After the taint and wilting of the garden
When our host of souls were few.
We were driven from the kingdom,
Expulsed by the wrath of Michael.
We followed the first of the fallen
Down to the world of man.

From body to body we grew by sevens.
As impure souls gathered to us,
Our evil new prosperity in Gerasene,
Until the martyred savior came.
He cast us out with his Father's light
In the cemetery by the Sea of Galilee.

Cruelly we stalked the holy land.
Unsettling the minds of the faithful,
Until the millennium gifted us a new host.
You find comfort in His existence,
But to acknowledge Him is to acknowledge
A thousand evil souls who dwell among you.

Ghosts Of You And Me

I said my last and needed goodbyes
Made peace with our bitter past.
Of all the faces that have haunted me
I'm resolved yours will be the last.

I left your part in my life behind.
The wronging of each other was all it took
To stop turning the pages of our story
And close our battered book.

It was always easier to say farewell
Than it was for me to stay.
You of all people would understand,
Did he give you the moon yet… did they?

Enough, no more reflections,
I'll lay the memory of you to rest in me.
No more hollow gestures or promises,
No more ghosts of you and me.

Anam Cara

Lights in windows gradually dim and die
As the starry firmament fills the sky.
A world's grown weary and gone to bed,
Disconsolate he stays up instead.
Wandering the many starlit haunts,
Searching for the only one he wants.
For the woman he would call his own,
A displaced dream of flesh and bone.

Vagrant of sleeplessness marches on.
He listens to the night's hushed sigh
Through the swaying trees and chimes,
Which play their lonely song for him.
What would he give
To hold her outside dream's realm?
Beyond that twilight world seen sometimes,
In reflections captured in dark, still waters, if only for tonight.

The stars in a deepest of dark blue sky glow,
Moonlit heavens mirror a work of Van Gough.
Art wasted on the same nocturnal story retold
Of no dusky gaze to meet nor soft hand to hold.
The fates look down from their starry perch,
Unwilling to aid in his desperate search.
But this is obsession that cannot be denied,
In untiring defiance he seeks his place at her side.

What would he give
To see her appear from the shadows?
Hear her step amid the scrape and scratch,
Of leaves tumbling down an empty street.
What would he give to see
Her silhouette in an orange pool of light?
To know the peace of her arms
And long forgotten sleep, if only for tonight.

The Walk

The moon rises slowly,
The glow it gives so pale.
Illuminating misty clouds
That act like a veil.

Stars begin to appear,
Pin-pricks in the night's veil.
They light the heavens
Every evening without fail.

The breeze is soft,
Rustling flowers left on hallow ground.
Hoot of owl, howl of wolf
Complete the chorus of nocturnal sound.

Gazing upon still water,
In the reflection stars shimmer.
Peering into shadowed woods
Where eyes of night creatures glimmer.

Wandering among the graves,
I listen to the spirits talk.
Enjoying their company
I invite them for the walk...

Dryad's Smile

I see her there
In a shimmering white dress.
Her bare feet walking
Atop moss covered earth.
And with each of her strides
Flowers spring in her wake.
Her skin is beautifully bronzed
By the sunshine upon her.

Her eyes are a deep brown
And as I gaze into them
I become lost in thoughts
Of running my fingers through
The golden tresses of her hair.
She notices me and smiles
With thin, pink, rosy lips
I crave to press against my own.

White blossoms rain around her
As she walks slowly over to me,
And lovingly holds my face
With her small delicate hands.
My fingers reach out to her cheek
She touches me to know what I feel,
While I touch her to see if she's real
This fantasy that smiles at me.

The Sea, She, and The Sailor

The Sea has come between them before.
A mistress that seduces the Sailor with
Tides leading to jeopardy and fortune.
This same scene has played out before.

She will stand alone. Hauntingly beautiful,
Waiting by the Sea. Her white dress and
Sand colored hair billowing in the breeze.
Her longing gaze on the ship sailing away.

The Sailor will rest a gold ringed hand upon
The wooden railing of his ship. Unfurled sails
Fill with wind. Taking him further from
The shore and the woman watching him there.

At Wars' End

There is always a price
For the victories won
That we don't often realize
When the war has begun.

Yes, the price is high
And we deal with the loss.
Fate flips her shiny coin
And we accept the toss.

Was the sacrifice worth it?
Did we lose more than we gained?
Answers, are few in the aftermath
And not so easily ascertained.

I cannot walk away
With some peace of mind,
Because peace in all this
Is something I could never find.

Widow In The Window

A widow stands at her window
Staring into the darkness of night,
Fearing emotions and memories
Her slumber may incite.

She stays up to brave another night
Gnarled hands cover a wrinkled face.
The pain of remembrance too fierce
Of her beloved she cannot embrace.

Her husband, her only love,
Left her to fight in the war.
For a while the letters came in,
They are what she lived for.

But the letters stopped coming in
And she was left all alone,
Slowly realizing her only love
Would never be coming home.

The widow looks out the window
Praying for respite from her pain.
The tragic thing is
Only the mourning remains.

Control

Despotism force feeds fallacy, distorts reality,
Demand truth and concealed lies you will get.
Excuses supplied, your rights denied,
A consequence for those who relent.

Dystopian reality endorsed by lies enforced,
Freedom of will and expression not yours.
The facts erased and liberty disgraced,
They're only satisfied when you're on all fours.

It has and always will be about control.

Control of your fears,
Your dreams and thoughts,
Control of your beliefs,
Your hate and heart.

The powers that be, issue their decree.
We already know what they will say.
Tainted by greed, obliged to mislead,
It's just another scheme to get their way.

Through their stipulation and manipulation,
Your role is defined and engraved.
Their obsession with your suppression
Leaves you devastated and enslaved.

It has and always will be about control.

Control of your fears,
Your dreams and thoughts,
Control of your beliefs,
Your hate and heart.

Control...

PATH II

Voodoo Queen

She is the voodoo queen of New Orleans.
A black magic royalty whose beauty is obscene.
Breathing in her provocative perfume,
It's no secret she has entered the room.
In a black stretch, satin dress she is arrayed
Meeting your stare with eager eyes of jade.
Her sensuous form sits across from you
Stirring desire you are powerless to subdue.
She is a carnal mystery as thick as the bayou air
As if some pagan god has answered your prayer.
You think it is her that your heart adores,
But unknown to you the choice was never yours.
Dark enchantment thwarts your mind's meager defenses
Through the unseen cloth effigy controlling your senses.

In Her Grip

In an empty garden claimed by autumn,
The man feels her presence wash over him.
There's a smell. More accurately, her own
Scent of overcast skies and martyred dreams.
Despair. She held him for so long.
The man has read her grim palm,
Knows every line and crease.
He doesn't want to believe its account,
But knows it by heart.
He is her unredeemed captive.

All In Your Name

You gifted me the kingdom within you.
In fealty I will uphold this vow:
To honor and protect that domain
Standing vigilant in its defense,
Its safety the glory I seek to attain
All in your name.

With pride I wear your symbol
So all may know where I stand.
I will champion your every cause,
Take up arms when need arise,
Fight beside you without pause,
All in your name.

Within the sanctity of your embrace
I know the greatness of this realm.
It borders the lengths of your arms
The only home I have ever known
Which I shall shield from all harm.
All in your name.

My Shadow

My shadow spoke to me.
This was no delusion of
A tired, troubled mind.
It counseled in whispers,
I alone could hear.
Entwined around my soul,
Irrevocably part of me.

Friend and trusted ally.
My blackened aura served,
Always ready to heed my call.
In palpable waves of anger
My shadow would manifest.
Phantom hands soon grasped
On their own bloodied accord.

I found myself alone after
Driving family and foe away.
Only my shadow remained.
I realized then what I had lost
In this Faustian exchange.
I would fear no human again,
But lost all claim to being one.

A cursed wraith creature.
With no conflict to sate me,
I no longer had a purpose.
Nor did the ravenous spirit
Still housed within.
No words were left to be said
Between my shadow and I.

Suicide proved no solution
In liberating my damned soul.
My shadow would not release
Its undying stranglehold.
So in hellish torment we lie,
Because I trapped my shadow
In death forever with me.

The End I Wasn't Ready For

It really doesn't work that way.
Let's just be friends…What
Words to say? You don't say a thing.
Are you capable of anything
Other than a pitiful stare?

It's not dramatic.

This parting of ways. Was it
Supposed to be? All I have
Is this nagging feeling of relief
That I don't quite believe. It's clear to me.
Remedial knowledge of one's own heart is
Not enough…
Love.
The end I wasn't ready for.

Dance of the Dead

He holds the fiddle
And plucks the strings,
Playing ghostly music
Awakening dead things.

The rotting cemetery earth breaks
The corpses begin to rise,
Swaying their moldy arms
Shaking their decomposing thighs.

The corpses follow the fiddler
You can hear the rattle of bones,
As they delight in the music
While waltzing around the tombstones.

The dead they rejoice tonight
Lives restored when they were done.
A skeletal dance in moonlight
So they and the fiddler can have fun.

But dawn lights the horizon,
And the dark melody shall cease
From its magical influence.
The dead must have their release.

They burrow back into the soil
Fearful of the touch of the sun,
But the music will be heard again
When the day is done.

Child of a Dark Prometheus

I am a monster. It has been a life's work.
A result of your tireless, irrational cruelty.
Your wretched creation, tormented by
The life I once knew. A life forever lost to me.
Peace will be known to us only through
Our mutually assured destruction, my creator.
I will not be trapped as this monster forever.

A crooked path stretches behind me,
My miles of mistakes stretch on.
Inhuman decisions made against you remain,
Steps away from the memory of who I once was.
Someone who escapes me. I lash out again.
No longer caring about the blameless people
Who lie between us. As long as I get you.

The story is nearly finished. The angry mob
Approaches in the distance. Coming for revenge
Against a monster that ruined their lives.
You smile. We both know that they will see
You as a victim, no matter what you did to me.
People will remember me as the monster when
You were less human than I could ever be.

We Will Not Fade Away

Everyone tries so hard
To sum our lives up with a stat.
They try to limit us with numbers,
We refuse to live like that.

The lines they draw in the sand,
We will keep crossing every time.
So many boundaries placed,
But they cannot keep us in line.

All the predictions they make
And the decency they forsake.
Despite cheap shots they take
Right here we will stay.

Our fists are clenched tight.
There is no ending in sight.
Yet we will survive this fight,
We will not fade away.

We're done being oppressed
And it is clearly understood.
We will silence their lies and
Be free of their power for good.

We will not fade away.

The Damned Son of Abraham

Eternity is remorseless
Here beyond the east gate,
As I wander alone through time.

The punishment of His absence
Cannot equal the legacy
He irrevocably tied to me.

The first innocent blood shed
At the expense of my brother
Has become a crimson river
Flowing deeper through time.

The deadly sin I committed
Was the first of its kind.
How could I have ever known
The immensity of my crime?

The mark he placed upon me
Insures I'll be a surrogate father
To countless murdering progeny.

No crime fits this punishment...

Wheat Field with Crows

I found you.
You were in the very field you painted,
The wind sighed and the wheat swayed.
You lay still.
I gazed up into the blue sky.
Was your Angelic Trumpeter near,
Had the dark winged heralds arrived?
Neither of these did my eyes see.
Your conscience led you to this field,
And it was I who failed to stop you.
Melancholy fueled your brush strokes,
Spreading dark paints upon the canvas.
As it became clear what it was, I asked:
"*What does this mean to you?*"
You froze momentarily before answering,
"*Vast fields of wheat beneath troubled skies.*"
It was then you turned your head so I couldn't see,
The wound and the change in your blue eyes.

A Night in Avalon

Night falls upon eternal Avalon again.
She appears as the fog rises off damp grass-
A girl with pale, milky skin
Wearing a dress dyed a deep blue,
Its dandelion colored trim is frayed
And stained green from the grass.
Her bare feet splash in shallow puddles
All throughout the ancient apple orchard.
Its towering trees bear blightless fruit.
There is no wind in Avalon, the blossoms
Fall straight to the earth like a heavy snowfall.

Ahead rests the sarsen tomb untouched
By time and adorned with scarlet dragons.
The Resting place of the ruler who reflected
What was best in men, a lord who fell in battle
Fighting his illegitimate son on Camlann's shore.
Undying braziers light her way as she passes
One who was once King and shall be King once more.

She races under Titania's immense bower where
Rays of moonlight pierce the canopy of darkness.
Illuminated eyes dot the darkness like stars as
She repeatedly takes nervous glances behind her
Knowing someone is there, but seeing nothing.
Robin Goodfellow in merriment and mischief
Shadows her until she clears the bower.

She runs along the shore of the great moat,
Leviathan-filled waters, that surrounds Oberon's castle.
The malevolent beasts sleep soundly this night.
A small rowboat drifts across the still waters,
Its rotting wood consumed by algae-
A derelict to warn those of submerged danger.

Her tiny feet pad across the cobble stone bridge
As she enters the courtyard of Oberon's castle.
Its occupants slumber peacefully and resume
Beautiful dreams they had left the previous night.
She stops upon reaching the gem stone fountain,
A towering sculpture of Oberon carved by the ancients.

She sits at the edge of the fountain,
Skims her fingers through the cool water creating
Ripples that agitate and form a shimmering face.
The visage smiles and gives a wink, the girl giggles
As it spits playfully at her and dissipates,
Blending in with the rest of the water.

But the time for fun is over
The first rays of light paint the sky gray.
The girl sees this and smiles sadly.
Gradually thick morning fog begins to rise
And her body dissolves, joining the mist
That's burned away by the arrival of dawn...
Another night in Avalon has passed.

The Dawn

I leave her apartment around five.
Light my cigarette.
The sky is the sickly gray
That comes before dawn.

Winter whips at my coat.
My skin begins to tingle.
Shouldn't cut it this close,
I could never help myself.

Orange embers gather at the tip of
The cigarette just like a fuse.

The city is trying to come around.
A few lights turn on. A few cars go by.
I dodge a couple stumbling along
Disheveled in drunken happiness.

Keep moving. Take another long,
Nervous drag wishing vainly to be still
In her warm arms. Her warm bed.
I bite down hard on my lower lip.

Hurrying down the empty sidewalks,
I ignore the lampposts shutting down.
Faded lights winking out. It's strange,
Having all of time and no time at all.

Pale blue creeps onto the horizon.
I imagine her eyes.
Upon the wind, ashes from my cigarette are carried.
It's only then I realize I've stopped.

She has no place in my world, but
She's the only human thing I have.
The skyscrapers catch faint sunlight,
I toss the burning remains of my cigarette.

Don't expect this story to end well
With all roads leading to damnation.
Tell me as the dawn approaches
Would you fault me for what I'm about to do?

Those Good Ole' Times

Guilt is the legacy you have left for me
In lasting memories I will never forget,
Unable to distance myself from the role
I played in this history of regret.

While I stood aside in voiceless accord
You enjoyed your every damning deed,
Leaving me to justify the many indecencies
I was unwilling to concede.

Victims of our unwavering cruelty
Became a trail which marked our path.
I am reminded of all those grief stricken faces
Every time I hear you laugh.

I was as degenerate as you were,
Your lackey and spineless accomplice.
The time we spent together is time
I loathe to reminisce.

It is now known to me what I must do
To keep this consuming shame at bay,
Staring you in the eye my choice is made
An overdue reckoning comes this day.

You are the tangible past I can destroy,
The constant reminder of my cardinal crimes.
Your demise the only thing which can silence
My memories of those good ole' times.

A Devil's Lament

Saints have no place in a devil's head.
To believe otherwise is just a charade,
But sometimes it is hard to dissuade
Drinking the wine and breaking the bread.
Smell of sulfur. Gone with no word said.
It's known what choice a devil has made.
Prayers and psalms cannot persuade,
Against the brimstoned road ahead.
A hallowed light will struggle not to recede,
As choices are made on the paths of want and need.
Memories of the Saint are given some thought.
What would a life of sanctity have meant?
But innate nature governs what is wrought
And so begins a devil's lament…

My Redeemer

What Hell I have dragged her through.
This devoted conscience bound in flesh.
Rescuing me from fires of fault and flaw,
The flames of my failures sear her.
Irrationally she remains by my side still.
Faithful in her belief I will someday honor
All the promises I have yet to fulfill.
I caress her lovely face.
She is my guardian angel,
My would-be saving grace.

There is no abandoning this path I tread,
As it coils deeper into unyielding sorrow.
She's radiant in the darkness engulfing me,
My salvation that refuses to surrender.
She sees all the noble acts I would commit
Fall easy prey to the infirmity of my nature,
Victims of the failings to which I submit.
Her heart has not hardened,
As I seek forgiveness for,
Crimes that cannot be pardoned.

How can anyone remain so patient,
When given no reason to remain so?
Despite this battle being a lost cause.
She valiantly confronts my demons,
Always without reservation or pause.
She is my Virgil in this Hell.
I would be lost without her,
My last and only chance.
My Redeemer.

Just a shove

Where's my salvation,
Deliverance from Christ?
To forgive and forget
Seems their only advice.

Don't speak of redemption,
When clemency is forbade.
Don't tell me there's hope
When tyrants can't be swayed.

Drowning within despair's depths,
Hopelessness my cement shoes.
The colors of life draining away,
Becoming blackened hues.

Do not question what I say.
Don't look for answers from above.
We stand at the chasm of this world
And life is just a shove.

Boogey Man

I'm the pariah created to explain your every woe:
Economic recession, failing education, rising crime.
A malady senators promise to cure come election time,
But they never do and I am the only one you blame.
The manufactured monster in this rigged racial game.

All of you share that identical look of fear,
As the children you hold closer when I walk by.
Did any of you stop to ask yourselves why?
Or are you so brainwashed by ideologies you keep
So sure that our differences go beyond skin deep?

What it all boils down to in this melting pot
Are the things you still refuse to understand.
But why bother when it's easier to fear me?
Hey, America, I'm your Boogey Man.

Matryoshkan Prison

Where has all the patience gone?
Temperament and understanding
Are needed and absent from our lives.
People react angrily to their situations-
Rage blinds reason and compassion.
Imprisoned by acts of intolerance
I saw this from within my own cell,
Until I built the strength to free myself.
The bars of my own failings gave way,
Letting me see the cell I escaped from
Only released me into a larger one.
Liberating yourself from your own faults
Does not free you from the faults of others.

PATH III

Winter's Love

My love is her sorrow. My kiss is a curse
Upon my lady's lips. Chapped skin. Blood.
Her head is bowed to avoid my touch,
Nevertheless she rubs her numb cheek
Wanting it still.

My love is her sorrow. My embrace
Leaves her breathless and weak from cold.
She's feverish, she's trying to repress
Shivers racking her body from my caress,
Wanting it still.

Her love is my sorrow. She bestows
Affections of warmth I cannot return.
The renewal that is her love cannot spring
From my glacial heart, but I can't help
Wanting it still.

Outsider's Eyes

I catch the eye of the walking dead.
Glazed over pupils reflecting only
The colorless world they propagate.
I safeguard my wonder and questions
For a time when they will have worth.
If I can only escape this necropolis
With what color and light I have left.

And it came as no surprise
That they couldn't understand
The distant look in my eyes.
Over time I've come to realize
They will never see what I see
Looking through my outsider's eyes.

Condemned to an afterlife of denial
These undead worship only themselves.
They seek defilement of my reverence,
The destruction of all I hold dear.
In grim defiance I refuse their beliefs.
Days spent fighting to keep my ideals,
Are rewarded with untroubled sleep.

Their sanctuary is the next sunrise
Let me sleep, let me take comfort
In meanings clad in dreams disguise.
I'll wake from this world they despise
To stare down a real nightmare,
Meeting its gaze with my outsider's eyes.

Years spent lost in this wasteland
With only my enemies for company.
Have I done all I could to escape,
Would I not have found a way by now?
How much of what I love still lives?
If I could look with outsider's eyes into my own
What is it I would see?

It's Alright, I'm Alright

There was a time when you relied on me
To protect you from any danger or enemy.
True to the last, now a thing of the past.
I now wonder if I was mistaken,
Your distance has left my faith shaken.

I've been lying to you for a long time
When I reply that everything is fine.
To hold up my end as one you call friend.
But what good is the loyalty I provide,
When you won't let me stand by your side.

I can't see the you
When you refuse to see the me.
It's alright.
I'm alright.
Ignore this fist that's clenched so tight.

I remember the bond we once shared,
Now a memory I wish to be spared.
You don't understand, take my hand.
You allow all these shadows to surround,
While I question why *I* am still around.

Maybe I could see the you
If you could see the me.
I would believe in you
If you could only trust in me.
It's alright.
I'm alright.
Just ignore this fist that's clenched so tight.

Until I Awake

You showed up again while I was sleeping,
A feeling as much as a face.
You ask me all the questions
I would never answer if I were awake.

Your smile haunts my every dream,
Frees every unredeemed sentiment.
And a memory is given life,
It wouldn't have if I were awake.

In this place I belong to you
The way I never could. And I feel
The hold you have over my heart
Squeezing tighter until I awake.

Asking Why

Moonlight breaking through the evergreens
Illuminating the night with its silver sheen.
Two souls wandering the night estranged
Walking together though everything's changed.

Memories of friendship and love long lost
A romance shared but in time star-crossed.
Keeping their awkward emotions at bay
They are so close yet impossibly faraway.

Phantom emotion haunts the silence
Fearful they refuse to admit its portents.
They are quick to dismiss what's occurred
But in a shallow grave the truth has stirred.

Guardedly they clasp each other's hands
Aware of the absence of wedding bands.
Nostalgia grants a momentary reprieve
From the fears they had come to believe.

Tonight they will try to take comfort in a lie
Careful in their avoidance of asking why.
Remembering vows and promises of forever
Continuing their walk in moonlight together.

The Waiter

My expression contorts into a smile,
Disingenuous as the people I cater to:
The Tri-state Aristocracy. All the while
Uttering, "It is just for now. Relax."

Pride. It's becoming a foreign word.
Gibberish while wearing this Monkey Suit
Black bow-tie, white gloves, tuxedo shirt.
I cannot help but laugh.

I watch them converse and eat, wondering
What goes on behind the high-class facade.
They're using the wrong utensil for the course
But such truths aren't spoken by peasantry.

Dance, monkey, dance. The organ plays a tune
Coins clink in the cup, time to perform.
Give me the cymbals. Clash, clash, clash.
What a waste of opposable thumbs.

I snap back into consciousness and
The standard of the service industry.
I'm here to make their dining dreams real,
While I live through this nightmare.

If they can train a chimp to fly a rocket,
Can't they get one to serve tables, too?
I clear dirty plates, remnants of their food
Sticks to my fingers and I wonder....

In space can you hear a monkey scream?

Nihilo Ex Nihilo

From the frigid iced lined crypt
You pull my cardboard mausoleum out,
Eagerly extracting my tin lined coffin.
In burning resurrection, I awake spinning.
A face looks at me through a square window.
For two minutes I snap and sizzle, then Hell's Bells,
Darkness and the opening of a door.

It's you.
You.

I'm pulled from my scorched paper sarcophagus,
In defiance I spit my burning insides onto your hands.
I'm dropped unceremoniously onto a slab.
If I could, I'd smile. My life, Nihilo Ex Nihilo:

Hydrolized Corn Gluten Autolyzed Guanylate
Thiamin Partially Hydrogenated Disidium Inosinate.

When you eventually consume me, when I'm gone,
I'll have given you nothing.
See you on the other side.

Sun and Moon

Most people come here during the day.
The sun's warmth on their faces a reminder
They're awake. Unlike those they visit.
The slumbering untouched by the sun,
Blanketed in thick clover and green.

Sunlight is the attention of a love-drunk man,
He's obvious and emits tremendous heat.
His illumination is direct and purposeful.

Moonlight is fickle in what light she will shed,
She offers no warmth. Her light is like a woman
Whose intentions are known only to her.

I appear here during the night. Alone with Her.
In the company of the slumbering, drifting
Along the headboards of marble and granite.
I feel her steady gaze on me as I run fingers
Across familiar etchings in rough stone.

There is no place for me in a world lit by him.
Such warmth is wasted on the likes of me.
A transparent individual without any feeling,
I've chosen her. Moonlight shines for her own benefit,
But I'd like to think she's doing it for me.

It Looks Like Rain

I grew comfortable
With an overcast sky.
In the absence of the sun
I found peace.

Through the haze and gloom
I found my way.
Through the hardships
And the struggles
Threatening like rain.

It's known to me
It will be some time
Before I see the sun.
But I'm not afraid of the rain,
Not anymore.

Though a storm approaches
I won't be coming in.
I'm filled with this feeling
I've never felt.

...It looks like rain...

...It looks like rain...

The wind is searing.
I shield my face
With steady hand,
Through my fingers
I stare ahead
At the ominous horizon.

It's known to me
It will be some time
Before I see the sun.
But I'm not afraid of the rain,
Not anymore.

Lightning fills the sky.
The thunder roars on.
I have a sense of peace
I've never felt.

…It looks like rain…

…It looks like rain…

The Words

My thoughts have been about you lately.
A guilty conscious wages war in my head.
There's an imbalance between us,
So much that has been left unsaid.
You're someone so sensitive,
But at the same time so strong.
Letting me see other points of view,
Making me see that I can be wrong.
Reverently I remember this,
These memories I can't forget.
I know you need to hear me say it,
But I cannot say these words yet.
Why can't I say the words?

When you're around life becomes different,
Somehow everything becomes more relevant.
I realize I'm in need of things I never knew,
That these things can be found in you.
But through all the lessons you've taught me
And after all that you've done for my sake
My only gift to you is my gift of silence.
Why can't I say the words?

Still no peace or quiet in my mind.
Some part of me needs to give way.
For so long I've been haunted
By the things I cannot say.
You've done more than you should have,
I won't have you holding your breath,
Waiting for me to say the words
I'll end up taking to my death.
You deserve so much more than my sad gift of silence.
Why can't I say the words?

Tin Man

Take this. I have no use for it.
More burden than ever a blessing,
You exploit its weakness
Using it to control me through pain.
The last thing human about me,
Is the one thing I cannot bear.

Take this. I know what its loss means.
My metal skin does not fear your threats,
Your fists cannot harm me.
But the truth of your word hurts me,
Leaving scars the only place they can.

Take this. A remnant I gladly forfeit.
Freedom in this unfeeling armor
In exchange for one last pound of flesh,
Your only leverage was the only thing
Human in me you could call your own.
Take the last thing making you and me the same.

Free

The long road we walked ends today.
We have come from such a long way
Just you and I.
Looking back it's scary to see
All the doubt and adversity
We have overcome.

Now we can live the life we dreamed.
Knowing our time is now,
No more shadows, no more gloom,
Our view is finally clear.
And I can see
We are free,
We are free.

Feeling this sense of liberty,
Having choices and possibility,
The realization of our dreams,
No longer fearing the past.
Our time has come at last,
The life we fought for can finally begin.

Not all who wander are lost.
We lived by that cliché.
Lost our sense of direction,
But finally found our way.
And I can see
We are free,
We are free.

Pee Wee Gone Mad

The playhouse has grown eerily silent.
Something about it just seems different.
Jovial laughter of children is no more-
Pee Wee's gone evil to the core.
That's right mother fuckers
Today's secret word is murder.
Another corpse wearing a red bowtie-
Another victim of Pee Wee's has died.

Red bowtie around his neck
Pee Wee never gets respect.
There's blood on the tweed
Pee Wee feels the need.
Yeah, there's blood on the tweed
Pee Wee's going to make you bleed.

Go ahead and try to steal his bike.
When driven to kill Pee Wee will strike.
Polished white shoes stained blood red
Pee Wee dances to "tequila" over the dead.
His maniacal laughter echoes into the night
Filling innocent children with fright.
Pee Wee's big adventure has just begun.
Yeah, Pee Wee is going to have some fun.

MURDER
[Everybody Scream Real Loud]

A Redemption You Don't Deserve

Who are you?
Do I know you from somewhere?
Eyes boring into the mirror
Fail to recognize who is there.

This eerie visage
I continue to scrutinize,
Placing a trembling hand on
An image I no longer recognize.

I never expected this -
Eyes peering at me without regret.
It is all I have ever wanted to see,
But I cannot believe what I see yet.

Eyes not ringed in dark circles,
This face not contorted in pain.

What finally did it?
Tell me, because I don't know.
When did all the inner demons
Decide to get up and go?

I continue to stare
At my double in the glass.
With a desperate need to grasp
What I should just let pass.

There is no reason to believe
In redemption given to the guilty.
Something inside still lingers,
Something inside does not agree.

Though this reflection says otherwise
I meet its gaze solemnly.
Instilled disbelief clashes
With this image of me.

Eyes not ringed in dark circles,
This face not contorted in pain.

Unaware

We bear silent witness to the world we live in
Filled with ideas and thoughts we need to convey.
But sometimes these expressions go unvoiced
And that is what's wrong with the world today.

No one questions what once was
Ignorance is as ignorance does.
Acceptance is easily taken
When the truth it is forsaken.

Existence lived in a depression.
Meaning lost with every concession.
The human race becomes a disgrace,
The decadence we willingly allow
Becomes the failings we disavow.

Always quick to condemn, never to understand
We are thoroughly judgmental and demoralized
Thus becoming what others deem appropriate.
We find ourselves missing who we once were.
Why can't we change, why are we unaware?
Time wasted in lost cycles
Leading to sorrow, shame, and despair.

And it is knowing the whole while
We are continuing to live in denial—
Going along with what's been said
Free will is as good as dead.

Integrity sold and bought
Death to independent thought.
We're so worn that none mourn—
Immense is the price that is paid,
Tragic is this hell we've made.

Why can't we change, why are we unaware?
Time wasted in lost cycles-
Leading to sorrow, shame, and despair.
Why can't we change, why are we unaware?
Why do we refuse to look within
When the answers can be found there-
Why don't we even care?

Familiar Madness

Look into my eyes and you will see
Within them lurks insanity.
I have suffered the loss of my mind
And pose a threat to all mankind.

I cannot be blamed; it's not my fault,
There's no resisting this mental assault.
The voices – they corrupt and traumatize.
Familiar madness clouds bloodshot eyes.

Manic laughter, uncontrollable convulsions,
I'm overwhelmed with violent compulsions.
Sanity only returns in the horrid aftermath,
As I recall details of this latest bloodbath.

I'm a puppet of these depraved desires.
A pull of the string, a manipulation of wires,
And I will do whatever the voices decide.
Desecration, destruction, or homicide.

Though guilt stricken, I will not pretend
Having any intention to see my life end.
There's only one thing I can clearly surmise,
This story will end with someone's demise.

Grand Scheme Of Things

We wonder what will be with the passing of years
As time marches slowly and then rapidly disappears.
None can make any real prediction,
Existence is paradox and contradiction.

Some will find peace or equilibrium,
Others may run afoul of bitter resentment.
Some of us victims of despairs delirium,
Others anchored by simple contentments.

Between the forces of free will and fate,
Our turbulent lives are buffeted.
Within the confines of our mortal coils-
We struggle to know why we are created.

Too much and too little
Always and never enough,
This life is never ours to understand-
When the scheme of things is so grand.

The Ongoing Story of Death and The Wandering Jew

A wrinkled and weathered man walked up a steep hill in the hot summer sun. Atop the hill waited an old acquaintance sitting by a familiar stone table beneath the shade of an orchard tree. Most would feel a chill permeate their being at the sight of the hooded figure, but this man is filled only with longing.

Death:
After all these centuries you insist in playing this game,
When you know, without His intervention, the result will be the same.

Cartaphilus:
My hopes are few but, I loose nothing in trying
When your victory may finally mean my dying.
Besides old friend, I have time I need to waste
When one awaits the second coming there is no need for haste.

The Grim hood nodded. Cartaphilus sat down at the table, its top a marble board with ivory and obsidian pieces set and ready to play. The Grim Hood chose the ivory pieces. Skeletal fingers picked up and placed a knight in front of his pawns. Cartaphilus' deeply creased hand slid a pawn forward. They spoke as they continued the game.

Cartaphilus:
At first I was in denial of my curse
An unending damnation made only worse
By the Apostles and the Disciples spreading the story
All for the purpose of advancing His Glory.

Death:
Yes, like the traitor who betrayed Him with a kiss,
He's insured you're condemnation until his return or forgiveness.

Cartaphilus:
In the beginning I held hope for peace
That with enough penance I would be granted release.
A millennium later His need for punishment is not sated,
But I've manipulated events to bring about the end that I'm fated.

Cartaphilus slid a bishop across the checkered battleground, slew the Grim Hood's knight and removed the corpse from the field.

Death:
It's known you're in league with the Morningstar's Son,
Plotting to bring about the advent of Armageddon.

An emaciated hand moved a rook toward the just triumphant bishop and hastened its journey to Heaven.

Cartaphilus :
…Yes, I figured by now you would know.
Tell me, does the Grim Hood care to reveal how it will go?

There was only silence as the two acquaintances continued the contest. The ivory and obsidian casualties mounted steadily as the game progressed. Close to the conclusion, **Cartaphilus** with eyes toward the distance spoke softly:

You know, the memory of that day remains vivid with me still.
My mocking of Him as He carried the cross up Golgotha's Hill.
It doesn't fill me with guilt; I can say that with conviction
I know if it weren't me, someone else would bear this affliction.
Gradually, I've come to understand I was His pawn
Meant to utter my jeers and be cursed all along.

Death:
The path was put before you, but the decision to walk it was your own.
Fate is not without freewill, you've reaped what you have sown.
After all these centuries you still don't understand,
A greater power has always guided my hand.
I cannot deliver you from your fate...
For this game, just as all the others, has ended in stalemate.

The hooded figure and the table were both gone. In the orchard's shade Cartaphilus remained seated, staring for a long time into the once occupied space before him.

ACKNOWLEDGEMENTS

Jason Zapata would like to thank Jason Stershic whose tireless energy and encouragement made this project possible. Professor John Hill deserves many thanks. His courses at the University of Scranton were the deciding factor in making poetry a permanent part of my life. Thanks need to be given to Chris and Lyndsey Hughes for their aid. I also thank all my friends and family whose support helped make this book possible.

www.ingramcontent.com/pod-product-compliance
Lightning Source LLC
Chambersburg PA
CBHW060407050426
42449CB00009B/1929